Honey, I Shrunk My Anxiety

Pocket-sized Methods to
Improve Your Mental Health That
Are Simple, Tried, and True

KATRINA BUELOW

DEDICATION

To my family, and to Adrian. Thank you for your patience and
for your constant support.

CONTENTS

FOREWORD

There are a few things that I would like to establish before you read this guide.

1. These methods were originally written for young adults, from a young adult. They were written in a time of vulnerability, during the difficult process of fighting through anxiety and depression. Since I found these methods very useful in my climb out of an unhealthy mental state, I trust others (including adults of any age) will find them useful as well.

2. I am not a doctor or a researcher. Therefore, I did not add any research references to the methods listed. This doesn't mean I didn't look for and affirm my methods with research when necessary; the information I give is not misleading. However, this is a subject that demands empathy and there is great benefit in authenticity. I am telling you what I know not from cold statistics, but from tried and true raw experience.

3. Despite my not researching the efficacy of these methods, I can ensure that if you decide to follow through with them with a true effort, they will work for you and you will succeed in improving your mental health.*

4. While I wrote these methods specifically for the purpose of fighting anxiety and depression, they work for a whole range of negative emotions. Under each method, I list which negative emotions the method will especially work towards improving. These include anger, anxiety, depression, despair, frustration,

irritability, loneliness, overall well-being, panic, sadness, stress, and "everything in between."

5. I realize that there may be a temptation to flip through this book quickly in order that you find the best fix in the shortest amount of time. I advise against this. Nothing worth fighting for comes quickly. This book is meant to be a journey, and after you've finished that journey, it may be used as a reference. My suggestions are that you read these methods one at a time (and never more than one per day) and that you practice only one per week. This ensures that you don't overwhelm yourself, and that you are able to really grasp and master the methods that will help you the most.

6. Good luck, and God be with you. There is hope ahead.

* If you have been officially diagnosed with depression, or feel you have severe depression, this book may not provide adequate help. I encourage you to seek out a counselor or therapist. This is not something to be ashamed of. Having someone listen to you more in-depth is extremely beneficial.

THE IMMEDIATE MOMENT

Physical Help

Breathing
(for anger, anxiety, panic, stress)

Above all, keep breathing. In every situation, knowing how to breathe will gain you control.

Try this.
1. Inhale through your nose, counting to ten.
2. Pause briefly.
3. Exhale through your nose, counting to ten.
4. Repeat nine more times.

When things seem out of control, know that you can control your breath.

"Calming the Baby"
(for anxiety, depression, panic, stress)

Extreme emotions can make you feel very vulnerable; they take away your calm, comfort, and control. You can reclaim these things back by treating yourself delicately, as if you were a frightened baby.

Examples on how to do this:
1. Hold yourself. Wrap yourself in your arms as if to remind yourself that you are present, and you are cared for.
2. Shush yourself. Your mind is trying to take over through its relentless attacks. Tell it, shhhh, over and over, until it listens.

Indulge your need to be treated as if you don't have so much responsibility. Let yourself release the pressure to be in control.

Smiling
(for anxiety, depression, despair, frustration, loneliness,
overall well-being, sadness, stress)

This is something that you often have to swallow your pride to do, because negative emotions do not want you to smile. It feels as if they will certainly not let you do so.

Go ahead and defy them.

Smiling has an amazing way of tricking your brain to let go of the negative. Smiling will lead to an automatic response which will, if you allow it, help you to list what might be going right, rather than what is going wrong. It's going to remind you about the hope you instinctively have.

Run with this glimpse of hope. It might be the ticket out of distress and desperation.

Silence Until Settling
(for anger, despair, frustration, irritability, stress)

Negative emotions do a great job of creating a desire in you to be mean, hateful, and careless. The problem is that you, when you are your happiest self, are not mean, hateful, or careless when it comes to your loved ones or to yourself. In order to maintain who you are and how you want to treat those around you, it's best not to vent when you feel that anger, frustration, or stress is taking over.

Expressing the negative emotions that you are suffering from will trap you into the mindset that they are in control of you and how you act.

Remember instead: your emotions are not in control.

By keeping silent about the negative thoughts that are flooding your mind, you are stripping them of their power.

When your mind has settled, your thoughts will likely be different. They will be more loving and hopeful, and will represent the better version of you.

Flexing
(for anxiety, depression, despair, frustration, panic, stress)

Whether this means showing off your arm muscles or smiling at yourself, get in front of a mirror and flex some muscles. This is a visual of you fighting back against your negativity.

This takes power away from your racing thoughts and gives it back to you.

You are in control, and sometimes you need a forced jolt of energy, and a visual of it, to be reminded of that.

Listening to Music
(for anger, anxiety, depression, despair, frustration, loneliness,
sadness, stress)

Listen to your favorite song or band, instrumental music such as classical or jazz, or a random artist with your headphones on or the speakers loud.

Music is a unique language. It might tell you what you want to hear, or tell you what you didn't feel like telling yourself. It may simply calm you down.

Succumb to listening to music instead of your emotions, and give yourself a break from your own thoughts.

THE IMMEDIATE MOMENT

Mental Help

Recognizing Your Capability
(for anger, anxiety, depression, despair, frustration, irritability,
overall well-being, panic, sadness, stress, everything in between)

Most methods in this book are about taking control back.
Control is one of the essentials to successfully managing your
mental health. You cannot change your past and you cannot
change how it may have negatively affected you, but you can
change how healthy your mind is going to be in the future.

It's time for you to realize that you are more than capable of
creating change.

The decision is in your hands to want that change, and to make
the moves that help you in your desperate times. These are the
ones which are going to keep you moving steadily forward.

You are capable of anything. Use that capability to take control
back, and to make this change.

Zooming Out

(for anger, anxiety, despair, frustration, irritability, sadness, stress)

Zooming out of your current situation helps you to externalize what is happening, and to control how you will allow the situation to affect you.

Here are some questions to help you gain this perspective:

1. What does this situation look like in comparison to your whole day? A whole week? A whole year?
2. What does this situation look like in comparison to what or who you care about the most?
3. What does this situation look like in comparison to what you have previously accomplished?
4. What is this situation alerting you to? What could you change in order to help this situation?

Looking at Your Accomplishments
(for anxiety, depression, despair, frustration, sadness)

This is for the times that you feel like a failure. Perhaps you've experienced another anxiety attack, panic attack, angry outburst, or bout of depression. Relentless and cruel thoughts are drowning out what is left of your happiness and your hope.

But remember that you've been trying, and working hard. Your lapse into negativity might have lasted a few minutes less than last time. Remember that you made a decision to try to improve mentally, and that this decision in itself is an accomplishment.

You have come so far, and you will go so much farther.

Acknowledging Every Feeling
(for anger, anxiety, depression, despair, frustration,
irritability, loneliness, overall well-being, panic, sadness,
stress, everything in between)

What you're feeling right now is important, even if it sucks. Ignoring it will ultimately make this feeling worse or prolong it rather than help.

Name your emotions. Capitalize them (Anger, Anxiety, Depression, Despair, Frustration, Loneliness, Sadness, Stress, Weird Feeling, etc.). Let them know that you see them and know that they are there. Hold them and befriend them briefly, if you like. Do not reject them.

Thank them for alerting you that something is off-balance in your life.

Kindly let them know that you do not need them anymore, because now that you know something is wrong, you can work to fix it.

Shushing Your Negativity
(for anger, anxiety, depression, despair, frustration,
irritability, stress)

You may have been told, "If you don't have anything nice to say, don't say anything at all." Although not always observed, it's actually very valuable when it comes to improving your mental health.

Speaking up on the negative comments that pop into your mind enhances them and gives them validation. It encourages and breeds more negativity.

Instead, shush your negative instincts. Swallow the urge to speak up on your negativity. Tell those instincts to go away. If you're feeling extra brave, think of something positive to say instead.

Surrendering to the Uncontrollable
(for anger, anxiety, despair, frustration, irritability, stress)

The emotions that this method will help with all have at least one thing in common; they are bi products of the desire to control.

It is crucial that you understand that not everything is controllable, and that is okay.

Here is a hands-on way to help yourself accept this:
1. Make one list of the actions, reactions, and situations you will reasonably be able to control.
2. Make another list of situations you cannot control.
3. On your list of Controllables, manage what you can. Make a plan to improve those actions, reactions, and situations.
4. On your list of Uncontrollables, acknowledge that you cannot control these situations with your own power. Then, give those situations to God, since He has promised to listen to every request you have, no matter what it is. Hold Jesus to his promise, which is to take our burdens upon Himself, and ask Him to take care of what you cannot change.

Listing Facts

(for anger, anxiety, depression, despair, frustration, stress)

Many of our negative emotions can find a way to create (very believable) lies. These might include comments about your supposed incompetence, your days and your weeks being worthless, your complete lack of anything good or hopeful, and many more. To clarify again: these are lies.

To combat these lies, get a pen or pencil and a piece of paper. Write a list of everything you know to be true. (Examples: your name, your age, your hometown, the color of the sky, the texture of the ceiling, the feeling of the pillow next to you, the number and names of siblings you have, etc.)

Facts are grounding and they are reliable. They can help your head to stop spinning with lies.

THE IMMEDIATE MOMENT

Spiritual Help

The Power of Prayer (Part 1)
(for anger, anxiety, depression, despair, frustration, irritability,
loneliness, overall well-being, sadness, stress, everything in
between)

1 John 5:14-15
"This is the confidence that we have before him: that if we ask
anything according to his will, he hears us. And if we know that
he hears us -- whatever we ask -- we also know that we receive
the things we have asked from him."

Philippians 4:6-7
"Do not worry about anything, but in everything, by prayer and
petition, with thanksgiving, let your requests be made known to
God. And the peace of God, which surpasses all understanding,
will guard your hearts and your minds in Christ Jesus."

1 Thessalonians 5:16-18
"Rejoice always. Pray without ceasing. In everything give thanks.
For this is God's will for you in Christ Jesus."

THE LASTING CHANGES

Physical Help

Journaling
(for anxiety, depression, despair, overall well-being, stress)

On good days and bad days, write down your situation, the events of your day, and/or your thoughts.

There is value in knowing that, on your bad days, not every day is bad. And on your good days, it is even more solidified that not every day is bad.

But here is something of even greater value: This is a way of taking control back, and of comprehending the events and feelings of your life more thoroughly. It will also allow you to make connections between your feelings and what might have caused them. This is very important not only for knowing why and when you feel upset or happy, but also for knowing what changes to make and where.

Staying Occupied
(for anxiety, depression, loneliness, sadness)

When you don't have anything to fill your day and your mind, your mind finds ways to fill itself. Too often, this means it fills itself with anxious or depressive thoughts.

When you're occupied, there is less room for the lies a bored mind is waiting to create.

While making sure not to overload your schedule (you want to have time to relax), try to add time for hobbies you enjoy or socializing with people you love.

Some suggestions to get your creative juices flowing:
1. Learn something new (a language, an instrument, a dance, etc.).
2. Clean or organize a room.
3. Write letters to friends, family, or to someone who will never read it.
4. Read a book.
5. Exercise or do some stretching.
6. Bake muffins.

Staying Healthy
(for anger, anxiety, depression, despair, frustration, loneliness, sadness, stress, overall well-being, everything in between)

Yes, this means proper exercise and diet.

Here are some reasons exercising will help you now and throughout your life:
1. It releases "happy" endorphins.
2. It gives you a healthy way to release negative energy.
3. It gives you a fun and easy way to take control in your life.
4. It's a chance to give back and be good to your awesomely-created body.

Here are some reasons eating right will help you now and throughout your life:
1. It gives you energy.
2. It's an opportunity for learning more about your body, and how it feels after eating various foods.
3. It's another area of your life that you can take control of.

Exercising and eating right are daunting habits that you might hear a lot about and do not want to take seriously. Here are a couple of tips to make them a little easier to take on:
1) Personalize these to you. Exercise in a way that's enjoyable to you, and simply gets you moving. Eat with curiosity, taking note of what feels good in your body and gives you energy, and what doesn't. Adjust accordingly, catering to your own unique body.
2) Understand that this is a very worth-it investment. It's a wonderful way to help you feel better physically and mentally, and helps you to thank God for your body and all it does for you.

THE LASTING CHANGES

Mental Help

Forgiveness (Part 1)
(for anger, anxiety, depression, despair, frustration)

First, it is imperative that you know that Jesus came to earth to live and die in your place. And he did it successfully. Because of this, God has promised to forgive you for everything that you've done wrong, ever.

You don't need to be afraid of acknowledging and apologizing for all of your sins and your weaknesses, of telling God about them and asking for forgiveness. Because after you do, you can believe that he has forgiven you for every single thing, for Jesus' sake.

After that, forgive yourself for your weaknesses. You can move forward now.

P.S. Now would be an excellent time to forgive others too, if necessary.

...

John 3:16
"For God so loved the world that he gave his only-begotten Son, that whoever believes in him shall not perish, but have eternal life."

1 John 1:9
"If we confess our sins, he is faithful and just to forgive us our sins and to cleanse us from all unrighteousness."

Focusing on Strengths
(for anxiety, depression, frustration, sadness, stress)

Find your strengths and be thankful for them (What are you good at? What have you done successfully in the past day/week/year?).

If you can't find any, you haven't tried hard enough. You have plenty! When you feel like you're not enough, remember and home in on those. They've served you well and helped you to get this far.

The truth is that you are competent. You have been equipped with many talents and gifts that shouldn't be ignored.

Work on being grounded in your strengths and even improving them.

Determining the Core
(for anger, frustration, irritability, sadness, stress)

Sometimes the lowkey, sneaky negative emotions are a danger signal. They might alert you to a bigger problem that you haven't discovered yet.

Examples:
1. Why are you actually frustrated? Is it because someone else is being annoying, or is it because you're annoyed at yourself for an action you regret?
2. Why are you actually upset? Is it because you didn't get to go out this weekend, or is it because there's a reason you want to avoid being at home?

Mental and physical reactions might be an indicator that there's an important area of your life that's not getting enough attention.

Looking at Loved Ones
(for anxiety, depression, despair, frustration, sadness, stress)

God has placed many amazing people in your life. Use them.

You can talk to family members or close friends for (at least) all of the following:

1. Your own clarification.
2. A detox of emotional buildup.
3. Their own understanding of what you're going through.
4. Accountability in your journey of mental improvement.
5. Support and comfort.

Take advantage of having people in your life that care about you (they truly do care about you). Use them for grounding and for motivation to keep going. And the more you improve, the easier it will be to love them in return.

Looking Forward
(for anxiety, depression, sadness)

Having something fun to look forward to is a great way to add some spice to your life, and to keep your spirits light.

Make dates with friends, family, or yourself. These could include lunch tomorrow, a movie on Friday, an ice cream party on Sunday, a bath next week, a personal craft, etc.

Be creative!

Reflecting
(for anxiety, depression, frustration, irritability)

In your spare moments, check up on how you're doing. This is a good way to protect yourself from potential emotional buildup or breakdown.

Think about how you've been feeling and how you've been reacting to situations around you and to life in general.

Remember what you've been accomplishing.

What is something that you could do today to keep moving forward?

Finding Joy in the Process
(for anger, anxiety, depression, despair, frustration, irritability,
sadness, stress, everything in between)

Making improvements in both body and mind can be extremely difficult. This is especially true if you are only looking at and comparing yourself to your end goal.

Here's the thing about mental improvement. It never ends! But this isn't a bad thing. It can actually be pretty exciting, because there are lots of discoveries to be made about yourself and what methods will work for you.

Appreciate the process that you're going through to improve. It's creating an incredible resilience within you.

You can simply trust that the results will come.

Having a Day
(for anger, anxiety, depression, despair, frustration, irritability,
loneliness, sadness, stress, everything in between)

It is more than okay to let yourself have a day to feel bad for yourself. Be furious, lay in bed all day, cry your heart out, scream into a pillow, watch tv all day. Whatever you need.

Improvement is very exhausting. Your body and mind need rest. Have a day to stop trying so hard.

The next day, though, you get to bounce up and try again. You had your day to replenish and renew, and now you have some saved up energy and motivation to try again.

THE LASTING CHANGES

Spiritual Help

Addressing Weaknesses
(for anger, anxiety, depression, despair, frustration, irritability,
sadness, stress, everything in between)

Here's a LIE: You are only worth something if you do well, or
are strong all or most of the time, or are good at most areas of
life.

Here's a TRUTH: We are human, and we are sinful. We have so
many weaknesses. But here's the hope… Where we are weak,
Christ was strong in our place. And God accepts us now, every
part of all of us.

What's amazing is that God uses our weaknesses to guide us to
search for solutions outside of ourselves. That's when we begin
to see how Christ is our only true strength.

…

2 Corinthians 12:9
"And he said to me, 'My grace is sufficient for you, because my
power is made perfect in weakness.' Therefore I will be glad to
boast all the more in my weaknesses, so that the power of
Christ may shelter me."

Philippians 4:13
"I can do all things through Christ, who strengthens me."

The Power of Prayer (Part 2)
(for anger, anxiety, depression, despair, frustration, irritability,
loneliness, sadness, stress, everything in between)

Keep praying, keep praying, keep praying.

Notes for the following passages:
"Righteous" refers to having saving faith (believing in Christ as
our savior).
Romans 8:26 refers to when we don't know exactly what to say
or how to say it.

James 5:13,15-16
"Is anyone among you suffering? He should pray… And the
prayer offered in faith will save the sick person, and the Lord will
raise him up. If he has committed sins, he will be forgiven. So
confess your sins to one another and pray for one another, in
order that you may be healed. The prayer of a righteous person
is able to do much because it is effective."

Romans 8:26
"In the same way the Spirit helps us in our weakness. We do
not know what we should pray for, but the Spirit himself
intercedes for us with groans that are not expressed in words."

THE MAINTENANCE CHAPTERS

Physical Help

Persistence and Practice
(for anger, anxiety, depression, despair, frustration, irritation,
panic, sadness, stress, everything in between)

Persistence is the key, persistence is the key, persistence is the
key.

This is going to make you push through the battles and win the
war. This is what is going to create true and lasting change.

Keep journaling. You don't have to do it all the time, but it is
useful for seeing your progress and for motivating yourself. It
can also keep you grounded in what the truth is about your
past, present, and future.

Keep working out. This is a non-negotiable, so find something
you enjoy.

Keep practicing the breathing. Practice it even in your calmest
and happiest moments, so that in your most horrible moments,
you know that you can at least breathe. This is something you
can control at all times, and practicing it at random ensures this
control.

THE MAINTENANCE CHAPTERS

Mental Help

The Influential Role of Desire
(for anger, anxiety, depression, despair, frustration, irritability,
panic, sadness, stress, everything in between)

It is crucial that you understand the following statement:

You cannot improve if you do not want to.

Your desire to have better mental health is always going to have to come back, no matter how many times you might forget about it. Keep some ways in mind to get your desire back if you struggle with losing it.

Sample questions to ask yourself to help you regain your desire to improve:
1. What do you want others to gain from you during interactions?
2. What else would you be able to focus on if you weren't struggling with your troubled mind?
3. How will better mental health help you to love those around you more effectively?

Bouncing Back
(for anger, anxiety, depression, despair, frustration, irritability,
sadness, stress, everything in between)

Falling back into your old and unhealthy habits is very
discouraging. But you can either succumb to the old you, which
might sink into that discouragement as a reason to be even
more upset, *or* you can realize that you have come very far in
your improvement, and wake up the next morning ready to be
the new and better you again.

It's called "bouncing" back because you need to jolt some energy
back into yourself. Re-motivate yourself and use the momentum
you had before the short lapse.

Gaining from the Past
(for anger, anxiety, depression, despair, frustration, irritability,
panic, sadness, stress, everything in between)

In the past, you had unhealthy habits that you needed so that you could cope with very difficult experiences and emotions. Thank your old habits for their service, and then stop looking at who you used to be as a way to bring yourself down. That isn't you anymore.

There are only two reasons that you should look to your past.

1. You can see where you used to be, mentally, and acknowledge the vast improvements you've made as awesome.
2. You can see what led up to bouts of negativity and learn from those experiences, and you can see what led up to times of elation and a positive mindset and learn from those experiences.

Forgiveness (Part 2)
(for anger, anxiety, depression, despair, frustration, irritability,
panic, sadness, stress, everything in between)

It's something that you have to do over and over again. As previously stated, improvement is a process that never truly ends because us humans are pretty good at messing up.

Understand that God has forgiven you because of Jesus.

Forgive yourself so that you can move forward.

Bonus points if you say "Jesus loves you, Jesus forgives you, and I forgive you" to yourself out loud. Extra bonus points if you say it in front of a mirror. It works better that way. Say it as many times as it takes to stick and make you smile a little.

Catering to You
(for anger, anxiety, depression, despair, frustration, irritability,
loneliness, panic, sadness, stress, everything in between)

Not every method you'll read or hear about is going to work for you. Or maybe a method works for you once, and not a second time. Some experimentation is going to have to occur (it's all part of the process).

Through trial and error, discover what works for you and fits the best in each scenario. Practice everything, and keep practicing the ones that work.

Keep in mind that this catering process will likely be continual. Because you're constantly evolving mentally, as you go through life experiences and as you work to shape your mind, some methods might work for a very long time and then not be applicable anymore. Then you get to find some new ones. Find joy in this process.

Persistence

(for anger, anxiety, depression, despair, frustration, irritability, panic, sadness, stress, everything in between)

It should be reiterated that along with desire, persistence is a total essential for improvement. You're going to have to practice your old and new methods for improving (a lot).

Persistence might be dreadful during the times you want to quit; eventually, though, you will be looking back and realizing that it all paid off. There is a lot of faith in this process. You need to trust that this is going to work and that more permanent changes are going to take place. Again, know that if you stick with the practice, the changes will stick with you.

Change does not happen in a day. It takes work and it takes practice (there's a reason for the saying, "practice makes perfect"). Understand that this work is totally worth it. Your happiness awaits you.

Preparation
(for anger, anxiety, depression, despair, frustration, irritability, loneliness, panic, sadness, stress, everything in between)

Lapses back into negative emotions are not ideal, but they are likely. It's important that you make a plan about how you'll react when they spring up.

If you make a plan, you won't be surprised when lapses occur. This lack of surprise adds to your control, which will help you cope and lessen your discouragement.

Your planned reactions should involve breathing and any method that's proven useful to you in the past. Don't forget to go easy on yourself if a lapse occurs. Accidents happen, especially during something as hard as working to improve mental health, and we get to learn from them.

Focusing Outward
(for anger, anxiety, depression, despair, frustration, irritability, sadness, stress, everything in between)

Your deeper motivation likely needs to come from a place outside of the happiness factor. Here are some questions to keep your motivation going when the improvement process is getting really old and really tough.

1. How is your better mental health going to change your treatment of others?
2. How is your better mental health going to change the whole nature of your relationships?
3. How is your better mental health going to change the way your days are run?
4. What goals are you going to accomplish because of your better mental health?
5. What do you want your life to look like?

TIP: After you answer one or more of these questions, create and go through with an action that reflects one aspect of your answer. In other words, do something today that reflects your end goal. (This might create some radical and amazing change in your life.)

THE MAINTENANCE CHAPTERS

Spiritual Help

The Power of Prayer (Part 3)
(for anger, anxiety, depression, despair, frustration, irritability,
loneliness, panic, sadness, stress, everything in between)

The repetition of this method is meant to emphasize its importance.

Remember the previous passages concerning prayer, and look for more in the Bible.

It is in the maintenance phase that praying might be getting a little boring, monotonous, or overall hard to construct.

At this point it is super useful to look at and read prayers that other people have written, so that you can say the right thing without searching in earnest for something to say at all. Awesome sources for these:

1. The Evangelical Lutheran Hymnary, specifically front pages 167-171
2. Christian Worship: A Lutheran Hymnal (the verses of the hymns)

A NOTE TO YOUR LOVED ONES

What Can They Do to Help?

In my experience, I have seen that family and friends are sometimes unsure on how to help their loved one when they are mentally distressed. For their sake, write or type a paragraph based on these guidelines, making sure to explain your specific experience and needs in dark times. I've written an example.

[Address your loved one.

Do your best to describe what negative feeling you experience; the feeling or feelings that you seem to drown in sometimes. Do your best to describe what goes through your mind when you're experiencing this feeling. Then identify how you might act in this situation.

Tell your loved one what you would like them to think and do in this situation that fits your needs best.]

[Dear Mom,

When I feel stressed or overwhelmed with anxiety, my mind races like it's going to explode and it makes me scared and absolutely hopeless. In those moments, I cannot see a positive light. I don't act like I want to when I feel like this. I become mean to you, and I want to yell and be violent.

In those moments, please be patient with me. It will be best if you take this moment to make sure I don't do anything violent. Please hug me and tell me that everything is going to be alright, and please do not give me any advice just then. I only need your presence and to be hushed.

Thank you for your patience and your love. - Katrina]

ABOUT THE AUTHOR

Katrina struggled with anxiety and depression throughout high school, its peak occurring at the beginning of her college career. As a result of this, her relationships with her parents, friends, and boyfriend suffered, and she was struggling to remember the last time she was truly happy.

Instead of waiting for a difficult life phase to pass, or using medication to dull the hormonal imbalances, she found a way to take back control of her mind while receiving video counseling. She has been practicing these methods to keep her mental health at its prime for two years and counting, helping others along the way by sharing her tips over social media.

She integrates a Christian perspective in her writing.

Contact her with questions, concerns, or comments at katrinabbuelow@gmail.com.

…

Many, many congratulations on finishing this book and on working so hard. I'm confident that you'll only keep improving from here on out. - Katrina

47611369R10039

Made in the USA
Lexington, KY
10 August 2019